GOD AIN'T
IN THE BUILDING

CARL ALLEN

God Ain't In the Building

By Carl Allen

Published by One Faith Publishing

Richmond, VA, Port Huron, MI

onefaithpublishings@gmail.com

TABLE OF CONTENTS

THIS BOOK IS DEDICATED TO...

———·⳾⳾·———

The ones who stopped going to church but never stopped talking to God... this book is for you.

The seekers who wanted truth more than tradition... this book is for you.

The ones who asked questions when silence was expected... this book is for you.

To every person who's ever questioned, doubted, or struggled with their faith... this book is for you.

To every Black man who grew up being told that emotions are a sign of weakness... this book is for you.

To every woman who prayed through pain, every child who sat in church confused but curious... this book is for you.

To every Black man and woman still healing from the lies that came wrapped in scripture... this book is for you.

I'm not perfect. I'm not a preacher. I'm just a man who got tired of pretending and decided to tell the truth.

If these words touched you, let them remind you:

You can honor your roots without being trapped by them.

You can love your people and still outgrow their traditions.

You can walk with God and still walk free.

And no matter where life takes you, the streets, the struggle, or the success… remember:

God never left. He was just waiting on you.

INTRODUCTION

THE TRUTH BEYOND THE WALLS

———·ᴄ♫ᴐ·———

I didn't write this book to start a beef with the church. I wrote it to start a **conversation**. For too long, I stayed quiet by sitting in the pews and watching people shout on Sunday and struggle by Monday.

I watched folks preach about freedom while still chained to fear. I watched leaders talk about faith like they had a trademark on it. After a while, I realized I wasn't losing my faith, I was **growing** it.

See, the version of God that most of us were given came with conditions:

Rules.

Guilt.

Fine print.

They said, "You can talk to God, but only through us."

"God will bless you, but only if you give."

"God loves you, but only if you follow my way."

And I believed that for a long time. Until I started asking questions that nobody wanted to answer.

Questions like:

If God is love, why does religion come with so much fear?

If He's everywhere, why does He only show up on Sunday?

If we're all made in His image, why are some of us treated like we ain't worth saving?

That's when my whole perspective shifted, and I realized religion wasn't built for freedom. It was built for **control**.

So, I left the building. Not to run from God, but to finally **run to Him**.

And what I found out in the quiet, in the struggle, and in the truth, it changed everything.

I met a God who didn't need my perfection to love me.

A God who didn't live behind stained glass.

A God who wasn't counting tithes but Who was concerned about me. That is what this book is all about.

This isn't a self-help book.

It's not a sermon.

It's a **testimony**…straight, unfiltered, and real.

It's for anybody who ever felt like the church left them behind.

For every person who ever loved God but didn't fit the mold.

For every brother and sister who's tired of religion telling them how to live.

I wrote this because I believe God's tired too, tired of watching His name get used for money, manipulation, and power.

He just wants a relationship.

He just wants honesty.

He just wants *you.*

So, if you're reading this, understand, this book isn't about walking away from your faith; it's about walking into your **freedom.** Because the truth is, God never needed the walls. We did.

But once you learn to hear His voice for yourself, you'll realize the real church was never a building.

It was **you** all along.

CHAPTER 1

SUNDAY SHOES & SIDE-EYED CHRISTIANS

———·❦·———

- ◆ *Growing up in church because you had to, not because you wanted to.*
- ◆ *Watching fake smiles and hearing holy lies.*
- ◆ *Feeling like religion was a trap and not a connection.*

I remember the smell of hair grease, cheap cologne, gospel music playing on the radio, and the scent of pressed clothes lingering throughout the house. That was our Sunday morning routine, and that was also the definition of "being raised right."

You see, growing up in Chicago, church wasn't a choice; it was **mandatory**. Every Sunday was like clockwork: put on your clothes, tie your shoes, and don't even think about talking back. Because if Big Momma said *we goin'*, you were

7

goin', and you better get your butt in that car with no arguments or excuses. The funny part? Nobody ever asked why. You just knew Sunday was *God's day*. We didn't question it, we didn't understand it, we just did it.

Back then, going to church was everything. The music, the hats, the shouting, it looked powerful, it looked like God was in the room. But even as a kid, I could feel something was off. Folks shouted loud enough to shake the floor but whispered gossip, judging, and frontin' before they could hit the parking lot. People cried at the altar, then cussed you out in the Fellowship Hall. It was like watching people play holy instead of *being* holy. I remember thinking, *If this is where God stays, He might need a new address.*

I was one of those kids who didn't just watch…I **noticed, and I saw too much**.

I noticed how the same deacon who told us to live holy was sneaking around with Sister So-and-So.

I noticed how the collection plate stayed full, but the single mothers in the pews stayed broke.

I noticed the usher board arguing behind closed doors.

I noticed how people were shouting one minute and living wild and gambling the next.

Something just didn't sit right with me. Even as a kid, I saw through the act because church felt like a show, and everybody had their role to play.

As I got older, I started asking the **'real'** questions that nobody liked. It seemed like everybody had faith in the pastor but not the Source.

"Why is the pastor driving a Benz but the members catching the bus?"

"Why do the pastors always get new cars but the same old sermon?"

"Why are we giving money every week, but the church roof is still leaking?"

"Why is it that God needs 10%, but He already owns everything?"

"Why do we give all this money, but the neighborhood still looks the same?

"Why do they say, 'Come as you are,' then judge you when you do?

They said I was angry and being rebellious, and I said, *I was just keeping it real.* No, I wasn't angry; I was **awake**. There's a difference. Anger reacts, but awakening observes. I've seen the church mothers judging girls for what they wore, even though half of them had their own skeletons tucked in choir robes.

I've seen the Pastor preaching and folks clapping like they didn't know he was talking sideways about half the congregation. That's when it hit me: **some people don't come to church for change; they come for recognition.**

And that plate? Man... that plate went around *twice*. The Pastor said, "God loves a cheerful giver," but I started thinking, *does God really need my twenty dollars, or do you?*

At first, I kept quiet. You know how it is; you don't challenge the church without catching some type of heat. But my silence started feeling more like guilt every time I watched people cry at the altar and still leave broken. I knew something was missing, so I started looking deeper by reading and learning where all this came from. Not the sugarcoated Sunday-school version...the real story.

I went down a rabbit hole and saw how religion had turned into a hustle, not always on purpose, but from habit. I also found out that religion isn't always about God. Sometimes it's about **control** to keep people quiet, scared, and loyal. If you keep folks feeling guilty or "less than," they'll keep coming back for more forgiveness.

That's when it clicked: maybe we have been trained to chase God through other people, pastors, bishops, and prophets, but the whole time, God was right there waiting for us to stop chasing and just **listen.** And deep down, that's when I stopped searching for religion, but for a **real connection**.

See, I'm not against God. I believe in Him heavily. And look, I'm not saying I'm perfect, I'm far from it. But I learned that **you don't need a middleman to reach God.** You don't need a preacher to speak for you, or a building to find Him because God doesn't clock in on Sundays...He's open 24/7.

Even after I found out some truths, I still kept showing up to church, out of respect, out of routine, or maybe even out of fear. But every Sunday, that inner voice got louder.

What if God isn't stuck in these walls?

What if He's been waiting for me to step outside these walls and find Him for real?

I didn't know it yet, but those questions were the start of everything. It was the seed that cracked open the ground I'd been walking on my whole life. From that day forward, I stopped dressing up for religion and I started **undressing for the truth**.

After that, I started going less and less to church. Not out of disrespect, but because I learned that **faith isn't about attendance, it's about your alignment with God.**

And once you start walking with God for yourself, you realize He doesn't need a fancy building, no collection plate, and no approval from man. He just needs *you*… raw, real, and honest.

So yeah, I still respect the elders, the choir, the traditions. But I don't live by it anymore. I found out that a relationship with God hits different when it's personal.

These days, I don't need a sermon to know God is real. I see Him when I wake up, I hear Him in my silence, and I feel Him when I make it through things I should've never survived. And that's why I say, you can love God and still walk out of the building.

Matter of fact, sometimes you've got to walk out to finally meet Him.

One day, I realized something powerful: Sometimes you gotta strip off the lies they wrapped around faith just to meet God face to face. Truth be told, God isn't looking for performance; He's waiting on your presence.

CHAPTER 2

CHURCH POLITICS & PULPIT
PIMPS

—·᷐᷍·—

- ♦ *Seeing the business side of faith.*
- ♦ *Pastors chasing money, status, and women.*
- ♦ *Learning early that most people worship the image, not God.*

Have you ever noticed how the church got its own kind of politics? Not the government kind, I'm talking about the behind-the-scenes foolishness that never makes it to the sermon.

The favoritism.

The backroom talks.

The ones who act holy on Sunday while on the pulpit but move dirty Monday through Saturday.

Once I started paying attention, I realized that the church got just as much drama as the block, except they just dress it up better in a three-piece suit and a long skirt.

You got the clique preachers:

The ones who only shout out certain people.

The ones who won't let you sing in the choir unless you're related.

You got the board members who control the money like they're God's personal accountants.

And then you got the pastor, moving like a CEO, talking about blessings but living like a boss.

I started calling it what it was…**Pulpit Pimpin'.**

Because that's exactly how it felt. Every week was the same thing: it was either a new series, a new message, or a new way to remind you that your blessing depended on your giving.

The pastor said, *"If you want a miracle, sow a seed."* But I started thinking, since when do miracles come with a price tag?

They made guilt sound like gospel: *"If you don't tithe, you're robbing God."*

Nah, I ain't robbing God, I'm just done with being manipulated.

See, real talk, some of these pastors learned the hustle from the streets. They just traded gold chains for crosses and learned how to flip scripture instead of flipping product. It's the same game but with a cleaner image.

I've seen it too many times, pastors living large while the congregation struggles.

Folks giving their last dollar but hoping God would pay their rent. But they're not realizing that their money is funding the pastor's next vacation or paying his car note.

And every time someone tries to question it, they get hit with *"Touch not my anointed."* That statement got more people scared to think or speak out more than sinning ever did.

One time, I asked a preacher straight up, *"Why do we gotta give money for God to move?"*

He said, *"It's about obedience."*

I said, *"No, it's about economics."*

And the wild thing? People are scared to talk about it and scared to admit that maybe, just maybe, the system ain't built for the people anymore:

It's built for **profit.**

It's built for **power.**

It's built for **image.**

It's built for **control.**

The truth? God don't need your money. He wants your heart. But half of these churches have flipped the script; they collect your money and forget your heart.

I'm not saying all preachers are dirty; some are real, and some truly do care.

But too many pastors got caught up in the game, the fame, and the attention.

"The Pastor said this," and "The Pastor said that," and before long, the message became about *the pastor,* and not about *God.*

That's when I had to step back and say, *"Nah, this ain't it."* God isn't a brand, and salvation ain't for sale. If you got to market Jesus like the new Jordans that just dropped, something is wrong with the product *and* the advertising.

So yeah, I still love God and always will. But I don't buy the foolishness anymore. I've seen too much, heard too much, and learned too much. You can't keep playing with God and expect me not to see the hustle or stay silent.

Because when you strip away the lights, the titles, and the fake love, a lot of these pastors ain't leading souls, they just running a business.

Somewhere along the way the church stopped being about salvation and started being about theatrics. It turned from a sanctuary into a stage. I used to think I was tripping or maybe I was being too judgmental. But the more I looked around, the more I realized it wasn't just me because other people were starting to see it too. They weren't losing faith in God; they were losing faith in the system.

How can you tell the people, "come as you are," but only love them once they fit their image?

How can you preach about humility from behind a thousand-dollar pulpit?

How can you claim to serve a God of truth and still be scared to speak it?

That's when I decided, I'd rather have a real connection with God in my living room than a fake fellowship in a church that's forgotten what the word *ministry* even means.

God doesn't need a spotlight.

He doesn't measure devotion by the size of an offering plate.

He moves through honesty, not hierarchy, and the more I stripped away from what was man-made, the more I started seeing what was God-given.

These days, when I walk past a church, I don't feel bitterness; I feel clarity. Because I finally understand, the kingdom of God was never meant to fit inside four walls built by a pastor's ego.

REAL TALK CHECK-IN

GAME RECOGNIZE GAME

Who did you once look up to, and when did you realize they were just human like you?

_____

_____

_____

How did the politics of church life make you question what's real?

_____

_____

_____

What's one sign you now watch for to tell the difference between leadership and manipulation?

_____

_____

_____

Reflection: Don't confuse a loud voice for an anointed voice.

CHAPTER 3

WHEN YOU START ASKING QUESTIONS

———·⌒⌒·———

♦ *The moment you stopped swallowing everything preached to you.*

♦ *Looking up history and finding out where Christianity came from.*

♦ *Realizing the "truth" they taught wasn't built for you.*

There comes a point when you stop taking folks' word for everything and start saying, *"Hold up… that don't sound right."* For me, that moment hit hard.

I grew up like most of us, believing what they told me because that's what you were supposed to do. *"Don't question God,"* they said. *"Just believe."* But one day I realized every time somebody said, *"Don't question,"* it was because they didn't have the answers.

So, I started digging. At first it was the little things, like:

Why do we call it "Sunday service"?

Why does the picture of Jesus on every church fan look like somebody who ain't from the same side of history as my people?

Why is every sermon about obedience but never about freedom?

Those questions opened a door that couldn't be closed. I started reading, really reading. Not the verses they cherry-picked on Sundays, but the stories they skipped over, the wars, the contradictions, and the politics in between. I went back into the history books and looked at how Christianity came here and how it got shaped to fit what America needed it to be. That's when the dots started connecting.

They took a book that was meant to teach love and twisted it into a tool for control. They told enslaved people, *"Obey your masters,"* while beating them bloody with the same hand that held the Bible. They preached about heaven while turning this earth into hell.

And for centuries, that programming stuck. It got passed down like a family recipe: *"Go to church, pay your tithes, be humble, and wait on your blessing."*

But after a while I started asking, "How long are we supposed to wait?"

See, knowledge doesn't come easy in a system that's built to keep you loyal and quiet. When I started asking those deeper questions about slavery, race, money, and how religion was weaponized, folks looked at me like I'd turned atheist. But I wasn't rejecting God, I was rejecting the middleman. Because the more I learned, the clearer it got: God was never the problem. **Man was.**

The history books shows that every time our people wake up, the system finds a new way to put them back to sleep. Sometimes with fear, sometimes with guilt, and sometimes it's with a smiling pastor telling you to *"trust God"* while he's trusting the offering basket.

And look, I ain't saying all churches are bad, but too many have forgotten the mission. They replaced spiritual truth with tradition and traded a raw and real connection for a well-rehearsed performance.

So yeah, I started asking:

Why do we keep praying for freedom when the chains have been unlocked?

Why do we keep waiting on heaven when God gave us a mind to build it right here?

Why do we keep calling ourselves "saved" when we're still scared to think for ourselves?

Once those questions hit, you can't unthink them. You start seeing the game for what it is, and that's when I decided to go straight to the Source.

I stopped letting somebody else interpret what God wanted from me. I started talking to God myself, sometimes in silence, sometimes in tears, and sometimes just riding late at night, music low, heart open. And every time, I felt His peace and presence. No collection plate. No choir. No middleman. Just me and God.

That's when I finally knew that faith isn't about sitting quietly and following the rules. It's about asking questions that lead you back to the truth.

And truth, the real truth will always lead you back to Him, and not them.

Because when you strip away the fear, the guilt, and the performance, what's left is the one thing that religion can't duplicate...**A real connection with God.**

And once you find that? You'll never let anyone make you feel like you need permission to talk to your Creator again.

REAL TALK CHECK-IN

NO FILTER

Write out the question that has been living rent-free in your head, the one nobody wanted to answer.

_____

_____

_____

How did people react when you asked real questions?

_____

_____

_____

How would your life change if you stopped apologizing for thinking deeper?

_____

_____

_____

Reflection: Curiosity isn't rebellion; it's about freedom knocking to come in.

CHAPTER 4

RELIGION & SLAVERY...
REAL TALK

———◦❧◦———

- *How they used the Bible to chain minds while they chained bodies.*
- *The mental and emotional leftovers Black people still carry.*
- *The difference between spiritual power and religious control.*

Have you ever sat back and really thought about how we even got this version of "faith" we're all supposed to follow? Like, who handed us this playbook and said, *"This is how you find God"*?

When I started digging into history, everything started making sense, and not in a good way. The same Bible they used to *save* our people was the same one they used to enslave them. Let that sink in.

Back then, they didn't just chain our hands; they chained our minds. They told our ancestors obedience was holy, that slavery was *"God's will,"* and that their suffering on earth would be rewarded in heaven. Meanwhile, the slave master was living in a mansion, praying over his dinner while our people were out in the field bleeding, hungry, and broken. That wasn't salvation, that was psychological warfare.

They picked verses that kept people quiet.

"Servants, obey your masters."

"Turn the other cheek."

"Blessed are the meek."

But notice they never preached the parts about justice, freedom, or how God led Moses to free His people from Pharaoh. Nah, they left that part out because freedom didn't fit their plan. And over time, that same twisted version of Christianity got passed down through generations.

Our great-great-grandparents didn't have the choice to question it because it was about survival. If they didn't follow it, they were punished or killed. So, they clung to it and passed it down to protect their children.

Now here we are, centuries later, still sitting in pews built on pain, and still repeating words that were never meant to free us. Don't get me wrong, I'm not knocking every church.

There are some real ones out there. But a lot of what we call *church* today still runs on that same old slavery programming:

Keep them loyal.

Keep them giving.

Keep them waiting.

Meanwhile, the same system that built slavery still profits off our pain, from prison to politics to the pulpit. It's the same cycle; now we're just wearing suits and carrying Bibles.

When I realized that, it hit deep. How can a book built on *"love your neighbor"* be the same one that justified whipping, hanging, and raping people?

How can you preach forgiveness to the oppressed but never accountability to the oppressor?

It made me mad at first, then it made me think. Maybe that's why so many Black men fall away from the church. It's not that we don't believe in God; we just don't believe in the version of God that they sold us.

The God I know isn't about control.

He isn't about guilt trips or fear.

The God I know is about justice, truth, and peace.

He's not hiding behind a pulpit, He's standing with the people.

He's in the strength of every ancestor who survived.

He's in the voice that says *"get up"* when life knocks you down.

He's in every man and woman who refuses to bow down to a lie.

Once you see that, you can't unsee it. You stop reading the Bible through the eyes of oppression and start reading it through the lens of liberation. You realize that maybe God never left us, maybe He's been waiting for us to stop living off someone else's interpretation and start hearing Him for ourselves.

The truth isn't comfortable; it's supposed to shake things up. And the day I faced the truth head-on was the day I stopped being religious and started being free.

REAL TALK CHECK-IN

BREAKING THE PROGRAMMING

What stories were passed down that kept our people quiet instead of free?

_____

_____

_____

Can you see any areas where faith has been flipped into a tool for control?

_____

_____

_____

How can you honor your ancestors' faith while still walking your own path?

_____

_____

_____

Reflection: You inherited their strength for survival and not their silence.

CHAPTER 5

501(C)(3) FAITH

———————

- *How churches run like corporations.*
- *The hustle behind "tithes and offerings."*
- *Why don't most preachers speak on real issues like slavery, racism, or poverty? Because their tax status won't let them.*

Let's be real, most people in church don't even know what a **501(c)(3)** is. They hear it thrown around like it's something holy, but it's really just a business license for religion. That's the part they don't talk about.

When I found out how the church really moves on paper, it blew my mind.

All this time I thought it was just about saving souls, but there's a whole trail of tax codes, money moves, and government rules hiding behind those hallelujahs.

A 501(c)(3) means the church is tax-exempt. Sounds good, right?

But here's the catch: that exemption comes with strings attached and rules about what you can and can't say from the pulpit, what you can and can't stand for publicly, and how quiet you have to stay when the truth might make the wrong people uncomfortable.

So yeah, they can't tax the church money... but in return, the church can't talk too loudly about injustice, race, corruption, or government lies. That ain't freedom, that's a contract.

That's why a lot of pastors tiptoe around real issues. They'll preach about heaven and hell all day but never about the system we're living in right now.

They'll tell you to pray for peace but not how to fight for it. Because the truth is, they got too much to lose if they make the wrong folks mad.

I started noticing that pattern years ago. Whenever something major happened, another unarmed brother was killed or the system playing with our rights, the same churches that once led marches suddenly went silent.

No outrage.

No call to action.

Just, *"Let's pray and have faith."*

Don't get me wrong, prayer is powerful, but faith without works doesn't change anything.

And then it hit me, they're not quiet because they don't care. They're quiet because they can't afford to speak up.

That's when I realized a 501(c)(3) isn't just about the paperwork. It's **control dressed like a blessing.** It's basically the government saying, *"I'll give you this money break, but you're gonna play by my rules."*

And the wild part? Most of them signed up without a second thought.

See, once you follow the money, the picture gets clearer.

The big megachurches, the TV ministries, and the pastors with book deals, they're not just preaching; they're running corporations. They got boards, salaries, investments, and PR teams.

Half the time, the church isn't owned by the people anymore; it's owned by the brand.

And the message? It's filtered now.

They preach what's safe.

They preach what sells.

They preach what keeps the donations coming in.

If your freedom to preach depends on a government form, then maybe you ain't preaching freedom at all, you're just performing it.

Don't get me wrong, I get it, running a church costs money. Lights, rent, sound systems, and staff, I understand the logistics. But when the business starts leading the belief, the message gets lost. That's why I stopped falling for the flashy lights, the big screens, designer suits, and fancy stages; that's not the anointing, that's **marketing.**

The older I got, the more I realized God never needed a 501(c)(3) to move.

He moved in prisons.

He moved in broken homes.

He moved in alleys, shelters, and backyards, the places the church forgot once they got air conditioning.

So now, when people ask me why I don't go to church, I tell them it's not because I don't believe. It's because I believe **too much** to stay quiet while the truth gets traded for tax breaks.

My faith doesn't need permission to speak truth. I'll take a real connection with God over a registered business in Jesus' Name any day.

REAL TALK CHECK-IN

THE MONEY TALK

When did you first notice that some churches felt more like hustle than healing?

_____

_____

_____

What does giving back mean to you when money isn't involved?

_____

_____

_____

List three ways to show love that don't cost a cent:

_____

_____

_____

_____

_____

Reflection: God don't need your pockets; He wants a one-on-one relationship with you.

CHAPTER 6

NO MIDDLEMAN NEEDED

---◦❧◦---

♦ *No more middleman between you and God.*
♦ *Learning to pray, hear, and trust for yourself.*
♦ *What it feels like when your peace comes directly from the Creator.*

At some point, you get tired of waiting on somebody else to translate what God's been trying to tell you directly. You get tired of the noise, the fake holy talk, the church politics, the guilt trips, and you start craving something real.

That's where I was at. I'd seen enough church games to last me a lifetime. I'd watched good people get used, manipulated, and shamed. I'd seen pastors with microphones turn people's pain into their profit. And one day, I just said, *"Nah, I can't do this anymore."* So, I stopped going through *them* and went straight to *Him*.

At first, it felt strange, like I was breaking every rule I'd been taught. I didn't have a pastor's approval. I didn't end my prayers with fancy words. I didn't have a choir backing me up. It was just me, talking to God like I'd talk to my brother, and I heard Him clearer than ever.

Nobody ever told me silence could be golden. That you could feel God riding in your car, sitting on your porch, or walking after a long day. Nobody told me the peace of God hits different when you're alone in His presence.

I realized God doesn't need an **appointment.**

You don't have to wait until Sunday to talk to Him.

You don't gotta shout to be heard.

All He wants is honesty, you, stripped of the mask, and speaking straight from your heart.

The more I did that, the freer I got.

I stopped worrying about sounding holy.

I stopped feeling guilty for missing church.

I stopped letting people make me feel like I needed their approval to be "saved."

Because the truth is, God doesn't live in buildings. He lives in *you*, in your struggle, your peace, your mistakes, and your comeback.

I started talking to Him everywhere, at work, in traffic, even mid-argument when my temper was on the edge. I'd say, *"God, help me see this situation differently."* And just like that, I'd calm down. Not because I'm perfect, but because I finally learned to let Him in.

And you know what's crazy?

The more I trusted that connection, the less I needed validation from people.

I didn't need a "word from the prophet."

I didn't need to stand in a prayer line to feel His presence.

I stopped chasing a feeling and started building a one-on-one relationship.

Now, don't get it twisted, I still respect the real preachers and teachers, the ones who live what they preach. But for me, I found my own relationship with God, my own lane, and my own language. Sometimes I write it down. Sometimes I just sit quietly and listen. And other times, I just say *"Thank You"* out loud, even when my life isn't perfect.

That's what going straight to the Source is all about. No middlemen. No filters. No fear.

Just you and the Creator, building a relationship that can't be broken. And once you taste that kind of peace, you'll never let somebody else tell you how to talk to your God again.

REAL TALK CHECK-IN

NO MIDDLEMAN NEEDED

Sit in silence for five minutes, no music, no noise. What comes up first: peace, guilt, or clarity?

_____

_____

_____

Write what you'd say if you could talk to God with nobody watching.

_____

_____

_____

What's one thing you're finally ready to say out loud to God?

_____

_____

_____

Reflection: Real ones talk to God directly...no middleman needed.

CHAPTER 7

CHURCH HURT... HEALING AFTER THE HOLY WOUNDS

———·⚜·———

- *Getting hurt in church hurts deep.*
- *Leaving church doesn't mean leaving God.*
- *Healing begins when you talk to God for yourself.*

Church hurt cuts deep, deeper than most people realize. It's not the kind of pain you can just pray away. It's personal, and it comes with layers. Because when pain wears a cross around its neck and comes *"in Jesus' name,"* it hits different.

When you get hurt in the streets, you expect it.

When you get hurt at work, you brush it off.

But when you get hurt in the house of God, a place that's supposed to be your safe space, it hits you in a spot you didn't even know could bleed.

The Pain Behind the Pews. I've seen people leave church completely messed up, not because of the Word, but because of the people. People were just looking for love, for peace, and for understanding, but ended up being judged, shamed, and judged by the same ones who shouted, *"come as you are."*

The church can be a **hospital**, but too often it becomes a **courtroom**.

Instead of healing people, they **sentence** them.

Instead of covering wounds, they **expose** them.

And instead of lifting each other up, they **step over each other** by trying to look holier than the next.

I've seen good people walk through those doors hurting and leave hurting worse.

They came for comfort and got **criticism**.

They came for grace and got **gossip**.

They came for truth and got **theatrics**.

Somewhere along the line, the church stopped being a place for the broken and became a stage for the flawless. But here's the truth: there are no flawless people. Every pastor, every usher, and every singer, they're all struggling with something. Some just learned to hide it better than others.

I used to think something was wrong with me, that maybe I wasn't *"anointed enough,"* or *"obedient enough,"* or *"holy enough."* But what was really happening was I was sitting in spaces where people were more invested in **image** than in **integrity.**

You could be dying inside, and they'd tell you to clap your hands and *"give God the glory."*

You could be drowning in depression, and they'd tell you to *"just have faith."*

But they never stopped long enough to ask, *"You good for real?"*

That's where the disconnect started for me because church became a **performance.** Some people didn't come to get healed; they came to **impress.**

And I realized that if I kept playing that same game, I'd lose myself trying to look saved instead of actually being free.

So, I walked away. **Not from God but from the noise, the judgment, and the manipulation** that made me believe that pain had to be part of my praise.

When I left the church, people said I was backsliding. They said I was *"letting the enemy get a hold of me."* But what they didn't know was that I had finally found **God for real.**

It was in that quiet place, no music, no preacher, no altar call, just **me and God.**

I wasn't looking for rules; I was looking for truth. And I found something powerful: **God never told me to depend on the church; He told me to depend on Him.**

I learned that the same God who can meet you in a sanctuary is the same God who will meet you in your living room, your car, or your broken heart.

He doesn't need lights or microphones to speak, all He needs is your willingness.

During my season of searching, I felt pain —

Pain from people I trusted who let me down.

Pain for the parts of me that believed the lies.

Pain for the younger version of myself that thought God's love came with conditions.

And then one day, I stopped feeling the pain, not because it disappeared, but because **peace finally showed up.**

That's when I learned the difference between **religion** and **relationship**:

Religion hurts you and tells you to pretend.

Relationship heals you and tells you to be real.

Giving Grace…I had to forgive, not because they deserved it, but because **I deserved peace.**

Holding on to hurt only gave them power over me, and I refused to let bitterness block my blessings. I stopped trying to fix what broke me, because you can't heal in the same environment that hurt you.

So, I took my faith, my hurt, my confusion, and I built a relationship with God.

Something not built on guilt, and something that didn't require perfection.

Now I know **church hurt shouldn't break your relationship with God.**

If anything, it exposes who was standing between you and Him. And once you move them out of the way, you can finally see the Source clearly.

A Prayer for Healing from Church Hurt

"God, I'm tired of pretending.

I've been hurt by people who used Your name for their gain.

But I don't want to hate them, I just want to heal.

Help me separate You from them.

Help me to remember that You never lied, You never manipulated, and You never abandoned me.

Teach me to love again without fear, to forgive without losing boundaries, and to walk in peace even when the pain tries to speak louder than my peace.

Restore my faith in You, and not in people.

Heal the parts of me that still flinch when I hear Your name.

I'm ready to trust again, not in the church, but in You.

Amen."

Declaration

I am not my hurt.

I am healing.

I am free to worship without walls.

I forgive what I can't forget, and I release what I can't repair.

My faith is not fragile; it's refined.

God still lives in me, and I still belong to Him.

No lie, no leader, and no betrayal can change that.

I am proof that peace comes after pain

and love always outlives the holy wounds.

Real Talk Check-In

From Pain to Power

Write down your church story, no filters. Who hurt you, and what did you learn about *yourself*?

_____

_____

_____

What does forgiveness look like to you?

_____

_____

_____

How can you keep your faith strong without allowing people to steal it again?

_____

_____

_____

Reflection: The same place that broke you can't be the place that heals you.

CHAPTER 8

HEALING THE BLACK SOUL

—·⋅⋰⋰⋅·—

+ *Unlearning the fear-based faith.*
+ *Finding strength in spirituality, ancestors, and truth.*
+ *Breaking that generational trauma of forced religion.*

Let's be honest, **being Black in America already comes with scars** we didn't ask for. Some visible. Most invisible.

We've been carrying the weight of generations, and half the time we don't even realize it. We got grandmamas who prayed through pain, mamas who worked through trauma, and men who never learned how to cry because they were told *"real ones don't show weakness."*

But nobody told us that **strength without healing turns into survival with no peace.**

See, we learned to survive everything, racism, poverty, police, heartbreak, betrayal, but somewhere in the mix we forgot how to just *be* who God called us to be. We forgot how to breathe and how to live without fear.

And when you look back, it all connects. Our ancestors were stripped of their names, their identity, and their culture, then handed a book that told them to obey. That conditioning didn't disappear when the chains came off; it just evolved. It turned into silence, into guilt, and into generations of people who loved God but were too scared to love themselves.

That's what I call **spiritual PTSD.** You see it in our homes, our schools, and even in our churches, because we're still trying to heal from something the world won't even admit happened.

For a long time, I was walking around wounded too.

Mad at everything but not sure why.

Mad at the system.

Mad at church folks.

Mad at myself.

Until one day I realized, I wasn't mad, **I was unhealed.**

That's the difference.

So, I started doing the work, not the *"just pray about it"* kind, but the *sit-in-your-own-pain-and-face-it* kind. I stopped running from my feelings. I stopped trying to look strong all the time. I started talking to God about the stuff I never told anybody, the shame, the fear, the hurt.

And little by little, I felt God start patching up the holes I'd been hiding.

Because **healing isn't loud.**

It's not a shout or a dance, it's quiet.

It's tears in the dark.

It's forgiveness when you're still feeling angry.

It's walking away from what broke you, even when it still feels right.

That's when I learned something that changed everything: **God doesn't heal what you hide.**

If you keep pretending, He'll keep waiting.

Because true healing comes when you finally let the mask fall and say, *"God, this is me. I'm hurting, I'm tired, but I still believe You can fix it."*

That's where **freedom** begins, not in pretending to be whole, but in trusting that He can handle your broken pieces.

And as I healed, I started seeing our people differently. I saw strength where I used to see pain. I saw power where I used to see pressure.

We are the descendants of the ones who refused to die.

Our existence is rebellion.

Our healing is a revolution.

That's why **healing the Black soul** ain't just about therapy or prayer, it's about **restoring what was stolen**: identity, confidence, peace, and connection with the true Source.

When we start seeing God through our own eyes, through our history, and through our resilience, that's when we finally start to rise again.

Because **God was never just in the sky; He was in our survival.**

So yeah, I'm still healing. Every day, I unlearn something that was taught to keep me small.

But I thank God because now I know what healing really feels like.

It's peace. It's power. It's remembering who you are and who you belong to.

Real Talk Check-In

Unchained

What's one lie you grew up believing about strength or faith?

_____

_____

_____

Who taught you to hide your pain, and what would it look like if you stopped?

_____

_____

_____

How can you start reclaiming your peace and your power today?

_____

_____

_____

Reflection: You come from survivors, but now it's time to live, not just survive.

CHAPTER 9

GOD AIN'T BROKE

- *Money, manipulation, and the guilt trap.*
- *Why giving doesn't have to mean getting played.*
- *Building a real relationship outside the church walls.*

L et me clear something up right now: **God ain't broke.** He never has been, and He never will be.

But if you listen to some folks behind the pulpit, you'd think heaven had bills due every Sunday.

Every message turns into an offering call, every prayer ends with a donation link, and every "breakthrough" somehow costs $99.99 with free shipping.

Don't get me wrong, there's nothing wrong with giving.

Giving is good when it's from the heart.

But giving out of guilt or pressure? That's manipulation, not ministry.

They tell you, *"If you sow this seed, God's gonna bless you double."*

But let me ask you, what kind of Father charges His children for favor?

See, somewhere along the way, we confused **receiving a blessing** with **being scammed.**

We started measuring faith by how much we give, instead of how much we trust God.

But God doesn't move in dollar amounts; He moves in obedience.

You could drop ten thousand in a collection plate, but if your heart ain't right, it's just money hitting metal. You could give your last twenty out of fear, but if you did it because someone guilt-tripped you, that's not faith, that's emotional coercion.

The truth is, **God owns it all.**

He doesn't need your checkbook to confirm His power.

He wants your trust, not your transactions.

And I get it, some people say, *"But the church needs money to run!"*

True. But that's not what this is about. This is about honesty, because there's a big difference between **asking for help** and **hustling the house of God.**

I've watched people give their **last dime to the church**, while hoping God would pay their rent.

People were taught to "sow in faith," but what they were really doing was **funding somebody else's lifestyle.**

The pastor pulled up in a new car while Sister Johnson was still catching the bus.

Something about that never sat right with me.

Because the Bible says, *"My God shall supply all your needs."* It didn't say, *"Your pastor shall supply all his wants."*

Somehow, we forgot that Jesus flipped tables in the temple when folks started selling. He didn't bless their hustle; He shut it down. So yeah, maybe it's time we start flipping some tables again.

Because the truth is, the real wealth isn't in a church collection plate, it's in the people. It's in the hearts that still believe, even after being lied to.

It's in the mothers still praying, the men who are still hoping, the kids who are still learning that God doesn't need their allowance to hear their prayer.

God ain't broke. He doesn't need your cash.

He needs your *commitment*.

Your honesty.

Your heart.

We've made performing appear better than acts of love.

We treat offering time like a talent show, who can give the most, and who can look the holiest doing it. But God sees past all that.

He sees your **heart**, your **intentions**, and your **sacrifice**.

If you give because you love Him, you're already blessed.

If you give because you're scared not to, you're missing the point.

God ain't broke, and He don't need a fundraiser or a chicken dinner sale to stay faithful.

He was blessing people long before a building fund even existed.

And the same God that fed five thousand with five loaves of bread and two fish can still multiply what little you have today.

So next time somebody tells you to *"sow a seed for a miracle,"* just remember:

Your obedience is the seed.

Your faith is the soil.

And your peace is the harvest.

When you trust God with your heart, and not your wallet, that's when you finally realize you can't buy favor; you live in it.

REAL TALK CHECK-IN

FAITH OVER FUNDS

When did you first notice that money was being used as manipulation in church?

_____

_____

_____

How can you honor God through giving without feeling pressured or guilty?

_____

_____

_____

What's one way you can give this week that costs zero dollars but comes straight from the heart?

_____

_____

_____

Reflection: God isn't asking for your cash; He's asking for your obedience.

CHAPTER 10

RAISING A FREE GENERATION

——◦⟨℘⟩◦——

- ◆ *Teaching your kids to know God for themselves.*
- ◆ *Building a faith based on truth, not fear.*
- ◆ *Passing down the truth, and not tradition.*

When I started waking up, I realized it wasn't just about me; it was about my kids, my people, and the next generation that's watching us repeat the same cycles and calling it **tradition**.

I don't want my sons and daughters thinking they have to beg for blessings.

I don't want them growing up scared of God instead of **knowing God.**

So, I decided: **I'm raising my kids with freedom.**

Freedom from **religious guilt.**

Freedom from **blind loyalty.**

Freedom to **question.**

Freedom to **learn.**

Freedom to **walk with God for themselves.**

See, we've got this bad habit of teaching kids how to *perform* religion but not how to *live* spiritually.

We tell them, *"Go to church,"* but we don't teach them how to hear from God for themselves.

We make them memorize verses but never explain what they mean.

We give them rules but not relationship, and then we act surprised when they walk away.

So, I flipped it. Instead of forcing my kids to know God, I showed them how to seek God for themselves.

We talk about God like He's family and not like some faraway judge waiting to strike them down.

We pray together.

We laugh together.

We question together.

Because that's what a relationship looks like.

I tell my kids, **"Don't let nobody tell you who God is. Learn Him for yourself."**

Because I don't want them trapped in the same fear I was raised in, scared to think, scared to ask, and scared to be an imperfect human.

I want them to know that **God's love ain't limited to Sunday morning.**

He walks with them in the classroom, on the job, in their mistakes, and in their comebacks.

That's how you raise a free generation, by teaching them that God ain't just in the church… **He's in them.**

Now, when I see my kids pray, it ain't forced, it's real.

They talk to Him like they talk to their best friend.

They love Him the way they know how to love. And that's enough.

Because once you break that idea that you've got to go through man to reach God, you start a whole new cycle, one built on **truth**, and not **tradition.**

And maybe that's what all this was for, the pain, the questions, and the disappointments.

Maybe it wasn't just about my healing, maybe it was so they wouldn't have to start from scratch.

So yeah, I'm raising mine differently.

I'm raising them to know the **truth** that I had to search to find.

I'm raising them to stand tall through it all.

I'm raising them to never lower their self-worth just to be accepted by others.

I'm raising them to always remember, **you can love God outside of the four walls of a church.**

REAL TALK CHECK-IN

CYCLE CHECK

What generational mindset do you carry that you know it's time to let go of?

_____

_____

_____

How can you teach the next generation to seek **truth** and not **tradition**?

_____

_____

_____

Write one lesson you want your kids, nieces, or nephews to learn from your growth.

_____

_____

_____

_____

_____

Chapter 11

My Peace, My Power, My Creator

—⸙—

+ Finding balance and strength in real spirituality.
+ Living your purpose without pretending to be perfect.
+ Closing declaration...*I went straight to the Source, and I found peace.*

You have to reach a point in life where you stop chasing approval from people and start chasing after your **peace.**

Not the fake kind, not the smile-for-the-picture kind, but that quiet, unshakable, deep-in-your-soul kind of peace. That's where I'm at now.

For years, I was running.

Running from my past, from pain, and from confusion.

The truth is, I was trying to find something that was already living inside of me.

I thought peace was something the church could give me, like it was a blessing passed from the pulpit to the pew.

But the truth? **Peace doesn't come from your presence being inside a church building.**

It comes from **God's presence** and from knowing who you are and who created you.

Once I stopped letting other people control my relationship with God and I started hearing from God for myself. That's when I realized my peace was never lost; it was just buried underneath the noise, opinions, guilt, and hurt that I didn't need to carry.

Now my mornings hit different.

I wake up and talk to God before I talk to anybody else.

No script.

No pastor's voice in my head.

Just me and God.

When you stop looking for a relationship with God through others, you start seeing Him everywhere…

in your breath,

in your laughter, and in those quiet moments when nobody's around.

Now *that's* my power.

Not money.

Not status.

Not titles.

Peace is my power.

And that kind of peace came when I finally learned to trust my own spirit, the same spirit that God placed inside of me from the very start.

See, people love to tell you what God told them *about* you.

But I learned that doesn't gossip…**He speaks directly.**

And when you're still long enough, He'll speak to you too.

God's voice doesn't always sound like thunder.

Sometimes it's just a thought that won't leave.

Sometimes it's the strength to walk away.

Sometimes it's that quiet reminder that you made it this far for a reason, and that reason isn't just to survive, it's to live **free.**

Free from fear.

Free from guilt.

Free from people who use religion as a leash.

So yeah, I love God, always have, and always will.

But now it's personal.

Now, it's about my **peace.**

My relationship with Him isn't about **religion** anymore; it's about a real **connection.**

It's not about rules, it's about **understanding.**

It's not about an image, it's about **intimacy with God.**

Because real faith doesn't need a stage.

It doesn't need lights or microphones.

It just needs **truth.**

And my truth is this:

God's been with me through every chapter of my life, even when I didn't know how to find Him.

He was there in my questions.

He was there in my anger.

He was there in my healing.

And now, **He's here in my peace.**

So, when people ask me, *"What do you believe now?"* I tell them this:

I believe in **relationship over religion.**

I believe in **truth over tradition.**

I believe in **freedom over fear.**

And most of all, I believe in a **God that lives in me, and not inside of a building.**

Real Talk Check-In

A Peace Plan

What situations or people have been stealing your peace lately?

_____

_____

How can you start protecting your peace without feeling guilty for it?

_____

_____

Where do you feel God's presence the most, in the noise or in the stillness?

_____

_____

What truth about yourself do you need to start believing again?

_____

_____

Reflection: Peace isn't the absence of problems; it's the presence of God in the middle of them.

Closing Reflection

"Straight to the Source"

———— ·⟨⟩· ————

I f you made it this far, thank you for real. That means you didn't just skip through these pages; you *read* them, and you saw yourself somewhere between the lines.

I didn't write this book to bash the church or tell anybody how to believe. I wrote it because I was tired of pretending that blind faith was the same as real faith. I wanted to talk about the parts of religion we're told to stay quiet about, the doubt, the hurt, the questions, the hypocrisy, all the things we whisper to ourselves but never say out loud.

I'm not here to destroy belief. I'm here to remind you that **God's been bigger than the building the whole time.**

My story isn't about rebellion. It's about **redeeming myself**. It's about breaking out of a spiritual cage and finding freedom in God's truth.

It's about realizing that you don't need permission to know your Creator, you don't need a middleman to be blessed, and you don't have to buy your peace or perform your praise.

All you really need is honesty, that's a raw conversation between you and God when nobody's around. That's where healing happens, and that's where peace starts.

To anyone reading this who's been burned by religion, judged by people, or made to feel like you're not good enough to reach God, listen to me:

You are, and you always were.

Because before you ever sat in a pew, before you ever learned a scripture, before you ever bowed your head, God was already there, waiting for you.

Thankfully, I found peace when I stopped chasing religion and started walking in a relationship with God. If this book does anything, I hope it reminds you that you can too.

Go straight to the Source and you'll find everything you were ever looking for...peace, power, and purpose is waiting on the other side of the truth.